Baby Animals of Florida

A fun, fact filled picture-book

Kathleen King

South Bay Publishing LLC

For Catherine Margaret, my sunshine

Book Design by MC Design Team

(Photo credits on last page)

ISBN 978-1-941952-05-4

South Bay Publishing LLC

Bradenton, FL

Printed in USA

Baby Animals of Florida

Retrostar

Welcome to the *Baby Animals of Florida* where you will have fun learning about these wonderful babies that live in Florida. Some animals may appear in other states but are closely associated with the state of Florida. You can get this book as an interactive eBook with pop-ups too!

At the end is *Test Your Knowledge Q & A* pages.

Baby Florida Panthers

Baby Florida Panthers are born with spots, but they disappear as they get older. The mother panther will stay with her baby until it is about two years old. The Florida Panther is endangered and is the State Animal of Florida.

Baby Panthers are 4 to 6 inches long when born.

Panthers eat mice, hares and alligators

Baby Panthers are called kittens

Panthers live in forests and swamps

A Baby Panther will grow up to be about 2 feet high

Baby Dolphins

Baby Bottlenose Dolphins are born in the water and live with their mother for 3 to 6 years. Dolphins can leap out of the water and 'walk' on their tails. They are the official State Saltwater Mammal of Florida.

Baby Dolphins are 3 to 4 feet long when born.

Dolphins eat
fish and squid

Baby Dolphins are
called pups or calves

Dolphins use sound
waves to find food

A Baby Dolphin will grow
up to be about 8 feet long

Baby Gopher Tortoises

Baby Gopher Tortoises are born golden yellow and turn brown as they get older. Because they get water from the plants they eat, tortoises rarely drink water. Gopher Tortoises are the State Tortoise of Florida.

Baby Gopher Tortoises are about 2 to 3 inches long when born.

Gopher Tortoises eat
grass, flowers and fruits

A Baby Tortoise
is called a hatchling

A Gopher Tortoise digs a
burrow 40 feet long underground

A Baby Gopher Tortoise will
grow up to be 9 to 12 inches

Baby American Alligators

Baby American Alligators hatch from eggs that the mother lays in a nest on the ground. The mother alligator carries the babies to the water in her mouth. She watches them until they are 1 to 2 years old.

Baby Alligators are 7 to 9 inches long when born.

Alligators eat fish,
insects and worms

Baby Alligators
are called hatchlings

Alligators are the
State Reptile of Florida

A Baby Alligator will grow
up to be 12 to 14 feet long

Baby Manatees

Baby West Indian Manatees stay with their mother for up to 2 years. Manatees can hold their breath for about 15 minutes. Manatees are an endangered species and are the official State Marine Mammal of Florida.

Baby West Indian Manatees are about 3 to 4 feet long when born.

Manatees eat sea
grass, weeds and algae

Baby Manatees
are called calves

The oldest Manatee is Snooty
at the South Florida Museum

A Baby Manatee will
grow up to 9 to 12 feet long

Baby Pink Flamingos

Baby Pink American Flamingos are born with white and gray feathers. Their mothers feed them a special milky food until they are 3 months old. Baby Flamingos will turn pink when they are about 2 years old.

Baby Pink Flamingos are about 5 to 7 inches long when born.

Flamingos eat very small shrimp and algae

Baby Flamingos are called chicks

American Flamingos live in Miami and the Florida Keys

Baby Flamingos will grow up to 3 to 4 feet high

Baby Cottontail Rabbits

Baby Eastern Cottontail Rabbits are born with their eyes closed. Their eyes begin to open by 4 to 7 days. Baby bunnies stay with their mother for about 2 months. Cottontail rabbits have a white 'powder puff' tail.

Baby Eastern Cottontail Rabbits are 3 to 4 inches long when born.

Rabbits eat vegetables
like lettuce and collard greens

Baby Cottontail Rabbits
are called bunnies or kits

Rabbits can live
up to 9 or 10 years

Baby Rabbits grow up
to be 14 to 17 inches long

Baby American Crocodiles

Baby American Crocodiles chirp inside their eggs to let their mother know when they are hatching. The mother stays with her babies until they are one year old. In the USA, crocodiles only live in South Florida.

Baby American Crocodiles are about 6 to 8 inches long when born.

Crocodiles eat fish
and some small reptiles

Baby Crocodiles
are called hatchlings

Crocodiles have webbed feet
to help them turn in the water

Baby Crocodiles will grow
to be 8 to 12 feet long

Baby Florida Raccoons

Baby Florida Raccoons are blind and deaf when they are born. Baby Raccoons start to see and hear when they are about 3 to 4 weeks old. The mother raccoon will stay with her babies for 5 to 6 months.

Baby Florida Raccoons are about 3 to 4 inches long when born.

Raccoons eat insects, worms, fruits and nuts

Baby Raccoons are called kits or cubs

Florida Raccoons live for 3 - 5 years and some 20 years

Florida Raccoons grow up to be about 2 feet long

Baby Burrowing Owls

Baby Burrowing Owls are born with beige and gray feathers which get darker as they get older. The mother owl will stay with her baby for about 12 weeks. Burrowing Owls live in open fields and cleared areas.

Baby Burrowing Owls are about 3 to 4 inches tall when born

Burrowing Owls eat insects, mice, snakes and lizards

Baby Burrowing Owls are called chicks

Burrowing Owls dig their own burrows 3 feet underground

Baby Owls will grow to be 10 to 11 inches high

Baby American Pelicans

Baby White American Pelicans are born in nests on the ground. When they are 3 months old they can fly. White American Pelicans have black feathers on the tips of their wings. Florida has white pelicans and brown pelicans.

Baby White American Pelicans are about 5 to 8 inches long when born

Pelicans eat fish and
sometimes turtles or frogs

Baby Pelicans
are called hatchlings

American White Pelicans are
one of the largest birds in the USA

Baby Pelicans grow up to 4-5 feet
and have a wingspan of 8 to 9 feet

Baby Mockingbirds

Baby Mockingbirds are born in nests that are made in trees. The mother and father feed the baby mockingbirds until they are about 14 days old. The babies are then able to fly on their own. Mockingbirds are the official State Bird of Florida.

Baby Mockingbirds are about 2 inches long when born

Mockingbirds eat
insects and fruits

Baby Mockingbirds
are call chicks

Mockingbirds sing many
different beautiful songs

Baby Mockingbirds grow
up to be 8 to 10 inches long

Crocodile

White Pelican

Dolphin

Burrowing Owl

Cottontail Rabbit

Florida Panther

Baby Animals of Florida

Manatee

Alligator

Gopher Tortoise

Mockingbird

Raccoon

Pink Flamingo

Test Your Knowledge

(Answers on next page)

1. Where does the oldest Manatee, Snooty (b.1948), live?

2. Where do Burrowing Owls live?

3. How big can Alligators grow to?

4. Where do Panthers live?

5. How do Dolphins find food?

6. When do Baby Flamingos turn pink?

7. What is the State Bird of Florida?

8. How long is the wingspan of the American Pelican?

9. What is the State Tortoise of Florida?

10. What is a Baby Raccoon called?

11. What kind of food does a Cottontail Rabbit eat?

12. Where do Crocodiles live in the USA?

13. Why do tortoises not drink much water?

14. What is a baby dolphin called?

Answers

1. Snooty lives at the South Florida Museum, located in Bradenton, FL.

2. Burrowing Owls live in open fields and cleared areas.

3. Alligators can grow to be 12 to 14 feet long.

4. Panthers live in forests or swamps.

5. Dolphins use sound waves to find food.

6. Baby Flamingos turn pink when they are 2-3 years old.

7. The State Bird of Florida is the Mockingbird.

8. The wingspan of the American Pelican is 8 to 9 feet.

9. The State Tortoise of Florida is the Gopher Tortoise.

10. A Baby Raccoon is called a kit or a cub.

11. A Cottontail Rabbit eats vegetables like lettuce or collard greens.

12. Crocodiles only live in South Florida in the USA.

13. They get water from the plants they eat.

14. A baby dolphin is called a pup or calf.

Baby Animals of Florida

A fun, fact filled picture-book

Kathleen King

We hope you enjoyed '*Baby Animals of Florida*'. If you did, let other kids know by putting a review on Amazon.com - or use http://amzn.to/1OGVDpl to get there fast! This book is also available as an interactive eBook with *pop up* screens for even more fun!

For more information, please visit my Facebook page at www.facebook.com/kathleenkingwriter. If you leave a comment there, I will get back to you.

Photo and Illustration Credits

Panther – Mazikab/Shutterstock

Cartoon Panther – Anna Velichkovsky/Dollarphoto

Dolphins – Blair Howard/Dollarphoto

Cartoon Dolphins – Anna Velichkovsky/Dollarphoto

Tortoise – Ryan M. Bolton/123rf

Cartoon Tortoises – matamu/Dollarphoto

Alligator – Stefan Ekernas/Dollarphoto

Cartoon Alligator–Anna Velichkovsky/Dollarphoto

Manatees – Nicolas Larento/Dollarphoto

Cartoon Manatees – Shanesabindesign/Dollarphoto

Flamingos – Worldswildlifewonders/Shutterstock

Cartoon Flamingo – davoor/Dollarphoto

Rabbits – Oraman/123rf

Cartoon Rabbit – AlexeyBannykn/Dollarphoto

Crocodile – chalabala/Dollarphoto

Cartoon Crocodile – tigatelu/Dollarphoto

Raccoons – Riverwalker/Dollarphoto

Cartoon Raccoon – Anna Velichkovsky/Dollarphoto

Owls – visceralimage/Dollarphoto

Cartoon Owl – meen_na/Dollarphoto

Pelicans – Anna Moskvina/Dollarphoto

Cartoon Pelican – lar01joka/Dollarphoto

Mockingbirds – Tony Campbell/Shutterstock

Cartoon Mockingbird - bluesky/Dollarphoto

Florida State Map – retrostar/Dollarphoto

Made in the USA
Monee, IL
22 September 2021